The Pattern of Sound Words:
A Study of Christian Beliefs

James Clifton, Ed.D.

ISBN: 9798584089627

Forward

This study is a result of an idea my pastor mentioned to me years ago. He told me we could use a good, in-depth doctrine study. A good study of doctrine might step on toes and could challenge personal perceptions and we decided that would be alright. People need to take a close look at what their faith is based on and should be able to do so in an adult manner, honestly discussing what the Bible tells us.

I developed an outline for the study based on what was "out there". I didn't believe I needed to create anything new. There are so many very deep, academic studies about doctrine. As a teacher, though, I eventually came to the realization that people don't want to discuss academic epistemology; they want to talk about faith. After months of reading, I decided to start over and form something like a basic outline that introduces doctrine and encourages it to be discussed. As an educator, it occurred to me that any study ought to involve the students, not just deliver information. The study was piloted in an interactive small group of church members over a two-month period. The process surprised me. The participants dug deep into their own experiences and perceptions of church doctrine as we progressed through the concepts. We had to draw the study to a close because it was consuming so much time. As it turns out, people do want to learn about doctrine. A large part of the learning process was comparing the different ideas people had about core issues of church doctrine. The pilot study showed me that people can be given a topic no one really wants to talk about and, if invited, can learn so much more from each other than any lesson plan can hope to achieve. If you decide to use this study, you will be creating your own unique discoveries about each other and about these doctrinal concepts.

If you are a born-again believer, truly forgiven, saved by the grace offered to you under the blood of Jesus Christ, you are a member of His family, a citizen of Heaven. As a citizen you have a responsibility to live your life according to the values of your heritage, which creates an imperative to know what these values are. These values are defined through doctrine. You need to know Christ, not just know *about* Him. As the Bible says, even the demons know about Christ. As a believer you are going to instantly recognize these doctrines, although you may not be familiar with their meanings. If you are not a believer, keep an open mind and prepare to face some facts. There is plenty of evidence "out there", but evidence can be misunderstood, misrepresented, misinterpreted. Evidence can, however, help you discover facts. Facts, once found, are incontrovertible, not something you can argue. Wherever you are coming from, long time believer, new believer, or believer to be, this study will help you gain some understanding of the basic doctrines of the Christian faith.

CONTENTS

ACKNOWLEDGMENTS

I would like to thank the group of guys who meet every Tuesday morning at our church for helping me with this. They agreed to set aside their usual agenda for several weeks to allow me an opportunity to bounce these concepts off of them and get some ideas on how to present the doctrines. The Mentors of Men were very involved and gave me some very good feedback. Wiser heads have certainly helped form the approach of this study.

I also wish to thank my wife, Sandy. She has done some publishing and is an excellent writer. Her reflections on this project have helped me avoid many errors, both in form and context. In addition to being my writing expert, she has also offered some invaluable insights on this approach to doctrine as a strong Christian.

INTRODUCTION

"If you are ignorant of God's Word, you will always be ignorant of God's will."

— Billy Graham

There are many cultures, many religions, even different versions of single religions

- Catholics, Jehovah's Witness, Church of Christ, Methodists, etc.; we all know people, family, and friends in these denominations, and we usually try to avoid talking about our differences. Most of the time we don't even attempt to talk about what we might have in common.
- Do you know why you believe what you do? When asked, can you explain it to someone else? Can you answer questions someone asks you about your faith?
- There are some absolutes. The postmodern era tells us "It depends", worldly philosophies erode basic Christian doctrine as they customize faith. Sometimes this is through an easily recognizable direct attack, sometimes by "adding to" doctrines, sometimes by classifying Biblical theology as "dead", "divisive", or "irrelevant"

We are living in, and may have been for some time, an era described in 1Tim 4 "…some shall depart from the faith, giving heed to seducing spirits and doctrines of evil"

From the same chapter: "For the time will come when people will not put up with sound doctrine. Instead, to suit their own desires, they will gather around them a great number of teachers to say what their itching ears want to hear." It's not like you haven't been warned, told that others will purposefully lead you astray. You need to know, to be firm in your faith and convictions…. basic doctrine.

The apostate church, that which has fallen away from original authority and in respect abandoned basic principles, exists in two ways. The first way is in their unwillingness to abide in the doctrine of Christ.

This has a lot to do with church organization. The second way is in doctrine itself, mankind trying to improve on God's plan. They just could not leave it alone; they had to interpret it for their own purposes. Just look at this short list of practices, introduced over these years, that have crept into doctrine since the early church.

- 120 – holy water, blessed by the priest, was introduced
- 157 – the concept of penance was created as a form of self-imposed agony to make up for our sins
- 593 – the idea of purgatory came around to free those who died without hope by paying enough money to the church to deliver those from torment
- 1000 – transubstantiation appeared claiming that through prayer the wine and the bread were changed to the literal body of Christ
- 1190 – the doctrine of indulgences was introduced, giving you license to sin as long as you paid the church a fee ahead of time.

These practices, and many more, worked their way into existence corrupting worship, confusing the body of the church, and further substituting the doctrines of man for the doctrines of Christ. It took 1300 years, a little at a time, eroding and clouding the truth, and is still occurring. N.B. Hardeman states "This ecclesiasticism is purely-of human origin. It is human in origin; it is human in doctrine; it is human in practice. The best definition I could render of such a hierarchy would be to say that it is a mixture of Judaism, paganism and Christianity." (Guardian of Truth, 1980, p.615) I heard a university research professor once say that if he was allowed to create the definitions, he could prove anything through statistics. People love to believe "evidence" that agrees with how they feel about something. Indeed, people will believe anything that agrees with their own opinions because it doesn't challenge them to face a truth.

Everyone here knows that if someone wants to convince you of something, they are going to tell you what you want to hear in ways that are comfortable to you. A radical notion is not sold by its departure from rational thinking, but by connecting it to your current thoughts as a better, or more modern perspective. You have probably heard that story about how to boil a frog. If you throw the frog into a pot of boiling water, it is going to jump out. If you put it into a pot of comfortable water and turn the heat up a little at a time it gets used to the changes and will allow itself to stay in the pot until it is too late to get out.

You know you have gone blind when you can see nothing wrong with something that God has called sin.

We have to have a working knowledge of sound doctrine to both defend ourselves and our families from the arguments of others and to clearly offer our faith to others as a way of salvation. A single person is poorly qualified to expertly interpret and expound on the details of theology. That is why we should study the word with other believers, to seek understanding, and to guard ourselves from misinterpretation.

Unlike some other religions, we are encouraged to seek meaning for ourselves from the Bible instead of being told what to believe. Flowing through the books of the Bible is history, poetry, law, and prophecy; all of these are different styles of writing. They are different styles, but the message is the same. In those books is a recurrent theme, a repeated message, one that is supported and proven in many ways. There is sound theology in most every book of the Bible. We are supposed to read the Word for ourselves, to be open to God's message, and to take part in the fellowship of other believers while seeking meaning from the Bible.

PURPOSE

Our salvation is directly related to 1) what Christ accomplished on the cross 2) what he secured by His resurrection, and 3) what He is doing in our lives through the Holy Spirit.

Let's frame our study on those three concepts and how they are related to our faith. Notice I did not say "religion". Religion is a man-made idea. It is a collection of rules, procedures, and creeds created by governing bodies of different conventions. This is why people are confused, afraid, or bored with the notion of doctrine. It just sounds like some old guys locked away in a secluded place protected by their intellect, unaccustomed to being questioned, out of touch with reality, insulated from real life. You and I experience real life, and we need the foundations of sound doctrine to be clear, relevant, and applicable. Personally, I have no use for those people, or groups of people, who want to fight each other over rules that have little, if any, foundation in fact or Biblical truth. Why do you want to waste your time over what men are arguing about if the solid word is right in front of you?

Our theology is strong if scriptural teaching is reflected in how we live with one another. This study will take a closer look at the deity of God, the life, death and resurrection of Christ, and the salvation it offers us. Then we will take a look at what the church is and what it is supposed to be doing. Let me offer you a topic sentence, a guiding precept, for each area we intend to study.

<u>God the Son</u> - We believe that Christ is 100% God and 100% man. He exists in three persons - Father, Son, and Holy Spirit - each being a distinct person with a distinct function but all of one essence and all possessing the same nature, perfection, and attributes.

<u>The Death of Christ</u> – We believe that the Son of Man was born to die in order to save sinners. He willingly offered himself as a sacrifice to pay sin's price that we might be presented to the Father without blame.

<u>The Resurrection of Christ</u> - We hold that Christ was buried, then literally and bodily resurrected three days later.

<u>Salvation</u> – All men are born sinful but may be brought from death to eternal life repentant of sin believing that Christ is their Lord and savior.

<u>Baptism</u> – Baptism is an ordinance, an act of obedience symbolizing the death, burial, and resurrection of Christ. In itself, it does not cleanse, purify, or otherwise save.

<u>The Lord's Supper</u> - This is the other ordinance we are asked to obey. Whereas baptism is done once, this is a repeated act of individual reflection to symbolize the sacrifice made on our behalf.

<u>The Church</u> – This is the organized body of believers brought together under a common faith and fellowship as the body of Christ on earth.

<u>The Church's Mission</u> – We have a responsibility to win, baptize, and teach all things to "the nations" commanded of the Lord. This is a basic commission given to all believers.

CONTEXT

As we move forward let's visit the authority of what we hold to be true. We ought to put the word of God into context, know where it comes from and gain some perspective on how it applies to our life.

The Bible - God gave His word to his people as the only authoritative standard for their faith and life. The Bible reveals truths about God and about what God does so that we may know God and have a relationship with God. Either we believe it is inspired and infallible or we don't. No other text in history has ever stood the test of time with respect to reliability, validity, or truth while constantly being studied by the foremost scholars of the world. We are quick to accept the word of "experts" in most every other aspect of our lives. Experts have turned the Bible inside out over thousands of years and continue to discover the same truths. If for no other reason, consider the prophesies, some 300 or so, that apply to the arrival and life of Christ. They all came true and stood the test of time for millennia. Nothing else has ever offered us as much undeniable proof, evidence, and fact. Jesus himself fulfilled 108 of what we call Messianic prophesies. The probability of this is one in 10 with 157 zeros after it. This number practically doesn't even exist. More on probability later.

It would be easy to say, "The Bible says it; I believe it; that settles it" and move on. The claims in the Bible either correspond to reality or they don't. As Christians we believe those claims to be true. To quote *Focus on the Family* "God exists, Jesus is not a myth, and the resurrection really happened." Historic credibility has been proven time and again. (Velarde, 2009) The Romans kept meticulous records. Roman historians Pliny the Younger, Cornelius Tactitus, and Suetonious all mention Jesus in their records as well as secular writers such as Thallus, Phlegon, and the Jewish historian Flavius Josephus (Goldberg, 1995). Even writers whose intent it was to detract from Jesus' works, Lucian of Samosata, detailed the events of His life, even the miracles. There is incredible physical evidence; there is inerrant consistency and coherence, and the reliability of its contents has never been equaled by any other volume. Jesus quoted the scriptures of His time as truth. If we believe in him, we must believe in the Bible. There is no question that Jesus is the most famous human being the world has ever known, with no armies, no wealth, no government, and only about a dozen faithful followers.

Science - Since the Enlightenment scientists have sought a natural, rather than supernatural, explanation of life and creation. Scientists accept that the universe is expanding and is the product of a singular event, a creation. Even Einstein had to finally admit that his theory of relativity pointed to a specific beginning. In that creation, for the universe to exist as we understand it over 100 conditions (gravity, essential proteins, minerals, and gasses, etc.) had to be met with precise accuracy. Nobel Prize winner and astrophysicist George Smoot explained that the precision required for these conditions to exist is likened to shooting an arrow from Earth to Pluto, four billion miles away, and hitting a bull's eye. (Witt, 2007) Another analogy I have heard is that, unless there is a Creator, prophesies of the old testament coming true are about as likely as a whirlwind rushing through a junkyard and assembling a 747 Jumbo jet. Mankind could never have predicted with that kind of certainty what would happen so many hundreds of years later without error. Most scientists are leaning toward the intelligent design theory these days. Such a belief must rely on faith rather than observation as there is no scenario based solely on science that could explain these events.

"Science without religion is lame; religion without science is blind."

A. Einstein

In fact, science has offered us the proof through statistical probability. Peter Stoner wrote a book, *Science Speaks,* that weighed the probability of certain events happening as they did as prophesied. (Reagan, 2018) His analysis was validated by the American Scientific Affiliation, which offered "The mathematical analysis included is based upon principles of probability which are thoroughly sound" In the opinion of the Affiliation, Professor Stoner "...has applied these principles in a proper and convincing way." Let me offer a few examples.

- The Messiah will be born in Bethlehem. (Micah 5:2) The average population of Bethlehem divided by the population of the earth at that time. 7150/2,000,000,000, the chances are one in 2.8 million

- The Messiah will die and have his hands and feet pierced. (Psalm 22:16) One man in how many has been crucified since the time of David in this manner? One in ten thousand.

- The money paid for the betrayal would be used to purchase a potter's field. (Zechariah 11:13) One man, in how many, would accept a bribe of this amount, try to give it back, and then buy a potter's field. One in one hundred thousand

- Seven prophesies by Ezekiel on the fate of the city of Tyre, just one example of what would happen to a city that denounced God. 1) Nebuchadnezzar shall conquer the city 2) other nations would assist him 3) the city will be made like a bare rock 4) it will become a place for the spreading of fishing nets 5) its stones and timbers will be thrown into the sea 6) other cities will be in fear at the fall of Tyre, and 7) the old city of Tyre will never be rebuilt.

The probability that just these few prophesies would come true, in this order, is one in 5.67 with 59 zeros after it. (Imagine the state of Texas shoulder deep in silver dollars, one of which has a black checkmark on it. Ask a blindfolded person to pick up the coin with the checkmark on his first try.) These prophesies were written a thousand years or so before Jesus was born and before the Romans started using crucifixion as a method of punishment. (Appendix) The point is, accidental fulfillment of these prophesies is beyond the realm of possibility. Regardless of what science tells you otherwise, this cannot be argued and strengthens the conclusion that He truly was God in the flesh. You are perfectly willing to accept as fact that there are 140 billion or more galaxies in the universe, that the earth spins on a 22.5% tilt and that electrons, protons, and neutrons exist but you have not seen these for yourself. The science experts tell you they exist. The Bible gives you first-hand accounts of miracles and the resurrection, but doubts linger because they are matters of faith, not science.

"The further a society drifts from the truth, the more it will hate those who speak it." G. Orwell

Consider the authority we accept when we reflect on our beliefs. Many religious beliefs are accepted without being understood. We accept religious claims because we have been told them since childhood but might be hard pressed to explain those beliefs. We defer to authorities on the Bible, on our faith, then on our denomination. We believe we should accept these beliefs, even though we can't explain them ourselves. This is not unique to religion. In the world of science researchers say their conclusions are based on fact; their studies start off with a set of assumptions. These assumptions are based on work others have done, shortcuts, deferences, or exceptions, whatever you want to call them. The same goes for economic specialists, political pundits, and sports fans. They follow certain veins of thought or reason to relative conclusions. (Bloom, 2015) The difference is, and this is crucial, the authority they place their basic belief assumptions in. As Christians we place, or should place, our sole authority on the written word of God. The scientists, politicians, economists, and tribal fanatics of sports teams place their belief systems in men. "The collective cultural activity of science, not scientists as individuals, most of whom prefer to be proven right, are highly biased to see the evidence in whatever light favors their preferred theory." (Bloom, 2015, para.17) The Bible isn't a collection of man's ideas, preferences, research, or opinions. It is the definitive word of God. Scientists are beginning to see the connections.

Instead of the Bible being outdated by science, we find that science is actually confirming ancient accounts of our origins. Everything, including time and space, had a one-time beginning. Our universe and planet are perfectly fine-tuned for life. DNA's sophisticated coding requires supernatural intelligence. Oxford professor of mathematics, Dr. John Lennox explains that the more we get to know about our universe, the more the hypothesis that there is a Creator gains in credibility as the best explanation of why we are here. (2018) Maybe we are coming full circle. We have tried our best to keep God out of our existence, but His presence is undeniable and inevitably the most pervasive influence on our lives.

Perhaps the best use of our time here is to study theology as it reflects in the doctrines of our faith. Theology is basically the study of God (theos – God, Logia – reasoning)

We can't study every concept, or cover every idea, or answer every question, but we can create the sort of approach mentioned in Isaiah 55, "Seed to the sower; bread to the eater". My task here is less that of a teacher than that of a fellow student of doctrine. I can merely present you with some topics based on sound theology and offer a forum of reflection. Paul told Timothy to "Take heed to thyself and unto doctrine; continue in them. In doing so you will save yourself and them that hear thee." 1Tim 4:16 If there is going to be a theme for this study, this might be a good one.

Let's move on from here and study, perhaps rediscover, our foundational doctrines.

"The true ground of most men's prejudice against the Christian doctrine is because they have no mind to obey it."

John Tillotson

Arguments against, and the need for, doctrine

There are any number of arguments out there that are used to undermine solid Christian doctrine. Those arguments are usually presented to you as an objection, some justification for not accepting, or at least diminishing the meaning, of solid theology.

The Bible warns us against the lies of false doctrine and false teachers.
1. Jesus warned about false teachers (Matt. 7:15-17).
2. Paul warned about false teachers (Acts 20:29-30; 2 Tim. 3:13; 2 Tim. 4:3-4).
3. Peter warned about false teachers and said that many will follow them (2 Pet. 2:1-2).
4. John warned about false teachers (1 John 2:18-20).
5. Jude warned about false teachers (Jude 3-4).

The Bible gives us some facts about doctrine.

1. The Bible is given for doctrine (2 Tim. 3:16-17).
2. We are to continue in the apostles' doctrine (Acts 2:42).
3. Preachers are to give themselves to doctrine (1 Tim. 4:13).
4. No false doctrine is to be allowed (1 Tim. 1:3).
5. Our doctrine is to be uncorrupt (Titus 2:10).
6. We are to separate from false doctrine (Rom. 16:17).

There are some specific false doctrines you need to be aware of and must confront when you can

Universalism: the belief that all people will be saved or that all ways lead to God and eternal life. Many who subscribe to this theology claim that, for instance, Christians and Muslim worship the same God.

The New Age Movement: a belief system of Eastern influence that emphasizes universal tolerance and doing what feels good (moral relativism). It contends that man is divine and can create his own reality and identity.

Legalism: the improper use of the law described in Scripture to try to attain or maintain salvation. Legalism also fosters judgment of fellow Christians for not adhering to one's own ideas of holiness rather than encouraging them to imitate Christ, obeying God's standards as explicitly outlined in Scripture.

Hyper-grace: the overreaction to legalism, resulting in abuse of God's grace. Believers find themselves drawn to the modern hyper-grace movement because they are looking for freedom not just from legalism, but also from God's standards.

The Emerging Church: a movement that claims to be Christian but employs culturally sensitive methods to make the gospel more palatable to a postmodern culture. Jesus' life is treated more as an allegory or narrative rather than a true event. Of particular concern is the inclusive approach to various belief systems, an emphasis on emotions over absolute truth and the notion that there is no hell, judgment or need for forgiveness. The Emerging Church movement also glorifies honesty and confession, but without repentance.

"There is a common, worldly kind of Christianity in this day, which many have, and think they have enough — a cheap Christianity which offends nobody and requires no sacrifice — which costs nothing and is worth nothing." J.C. Ryle

Behind all these false ideologies is the belief that Scripture is not infallible, and truth simply changes with the times. A 2014 Gallup poll (Saad, L. 2017) revealed that:

- 22 percent of Americans believe the Bible is the actual Word of God and should be taken literally
- 28 percent believe it is the actual Word of God, but with multiple possible interpretations

- 28 percent believe the Bible is the inspired Word of God but should not be taken literally
- 18 percent believe it is an ancient book of legends, history and moral precepts written by man

Just for your edification, and before we get into objections to doctrine and the need for sound doctrine, let me offer an observation on the New Apostolic Reformation (NAR). This is alive and well in a medium sized Texas city, and across the world, and you need to know about it. The NAR is not a church, although it is part of the One Church Unification movement. It is an ideology, a way of making sense of things for people who misinterpret the Bible, read between the lines, and create their own meaning. Let me repeat what Paul told us. "The time will come when they will not endure sound doctrine." Tim 4:3.

I recently saw a video of a service from a local church where two men professed to be prophets and apostles of God. They told the audience that if they would submit to their leadership that they too would work mighty miracles. These people claim that they have received God given authority, miraculous powers, and divine strategies to help advance God's kingdom in order for Christ to return. In short, if their leadership is followed, people can quicken the second coming. They admonish the crowd by telling them that if they do not follow them that they will miss out on the end time plans of God and that they have become a servant of the spirit of religion, not of the faith.

Leaders of this movement call it apostolic because they claim to be restoring apostles and prophets to the Church. They call it a reformation because they say church is not being done correctly, and that their movement will have more impact than the 16th century Reformation. There are over three million members in churches that follow this movement, and it is gaining momentum. Here is a site that will give you hundreds of books, articles, and journals defining and promoting the fivefold church. For further reading see http://www.deceptioninthechurch.com/newapostolic.html

If you have never heard of the five-fold church, then let me take you there. Based loosely on Ephesians 4:11 this ideology is predicated on the need for all five of these tasks to be present in any church that truly serves God "It was he who gave some to be apostles, some to be prophets, some to be evangelists, some to be pastors, and some to be teachers." Ephesians goes on to ad that these functions were needed "…so that the body of Christ may be built up until we all reach unity in faith…" Their bottom line is that since this has not yet been done, we must still need prophets and apostles. Let me emphasize the use of the word "unity" here. It is a defining concept of the New Apostolic Reformation movement. Just in case you missed it, the Pope stated to the World Council of Churches on Jan 16 of 2019 "Again, this year we are called to pray so that all Christians may once again be a single family, according to God's will 'so that they may all be one". (Vatican News, 2019) He is supporting the need and formation of a universal church. The Bible tells us to stand apart. In Romans 12:2 we see "Do not be conformed to this world, but be transformed by the renewal of your mind, that by testing you may discern what is the will of God, what is good and acceptable and perfect".

We aren't called to be like other Christians; we are called to be like Christ.

Ephesians 4:20 tells us that the church is "built on the foundation of the apostles and prophets, with Christ Jesus himself as the cornerstone." This begs the question then of whether we are still building the foundation. Heb 6:13 tells us to move on from the foundation. The role of the cornerstone is complete with His death, burial, resurrection, and ascension, so it follows that the foundation is complete. God's revealed Word was completed with the close of the New Testament. There is no need for further revelation. The Word is our guide, front to back, side to side, top to bottom.

Objections to the need for doctrine

Today there is a movement to turn away from the sound doctrines of the Word and cling to the philosophies of men. You can hear great speeches, read wonderful books, buy into strong sounding ethical and moral conclusions, and wrap yourself up in social gospel that tells that that the doctrines of old are dead and irrelevant. Borrowing from

Kevin Connors "The Christian Doctrine" (1995) let's look at five objections people offer to refute the need for doctrine.

Objection One: There is no Biblical record of Jesus or any of the apostles formulating or giving and formal system of doctrine.

Response: Acts 2:42 "They devoted themselves to the apostle's teaching…" tells us that the writers of the Bible presented the underlying theological facts concerning God in their books. The issues of sin, His nature and being, man and redemption, and other doctrines are in the Bible. If they were not, then we would probably not believe them ourselves.

Objection Two: The church does not need doctrine for doctrine has always been divisive and this is why there are so many denominations.

Response: Doctrine existed before the church existed. The church does not create doctrine. The Scriptures emphasize sound doctrine. A person who rejects Scripture, and God, is who causes division. It is often the case that the one who abuses, or misuses doctrine is doing so to cause division.

Objection Three: It does not matter what you believe; it only matters who you believe.

Response: It isn't possible to separate Christ from His doctrine; He and His word are one. You can't accept Christ and reject what He teaches. John 7:16/17 "My doctrine is not Mine, but His that sent me." If you believe in Him, you must accept His doctrine.

Objection Four: You can be right in your doctrine and wrong in your spirit and you won't be right with God, but you can be wrong in your doctrine and right in your spirit and be acceptable to God.

Response: This means that your attitudes are more important than sound doctrine. You cannot conclude that your intentions, even though good, outweigh poor doctrine. People can still be hurt by friendly fire.

Objection Five: Doctrine is dry, dull, dead, and useless for us today. Experience is more important than doctrine.

Response: Here is where it gets personal for me…doctrine may be dull and dry, but it is not the doctrine as much as it is the one presenting it. The life of what is taught is the life of the teacher. I dreaded taking a statistics course the first semester of my master's degree. I had a professor though, who made it real, who showed me application, who demonstrated relevance of the methods. Some of you may have had a teacher that did not help you connect to what was being studied. You may have, at a later date, had a teacher that made the information work for you. The material is all the same; the delivery is different.

There is lots of information "out there", some useful, most not. Information is used in the creation of knowledge, not just awareness. We educate through the mechanism of teaching, we teach through the lessons of experience, and we create knowledge by connecting relevance to application. Input - Process - Result

It is my hope that the way I bring this to you creates a desire to know more about Christian doctrine. I have learned so much working through this myself as I put this study together.

Need for Doctrine

We live in a world of relativism. Many people will tell you that right and wrong depend on the situation and that there are no absolutes. In the criminal justice courses I teach students about two kinds of law 1) *mala in se* and 2) *mala prohibita*. The first term represents crimes that are wrong because they are wrong just about anywhere, for example murder. The second represents crimes that are wrong because we have determined they should be, so we create a law saying so, such as requiring you to wear a seat belt.

Somehow, I believe that most people know when something is wrong because we have something in us that makes us feel it. The whole body of law built around "intent" is designed to determine the *mens rea*, knowledge of wrongdoing, of a crime. This is where we get to the slippery slope of "it depends" when people try to justify their actions. They knew something was wrong when they did it.

Absolutism is a concept that is deontological; it does not weigh the right or wrong of an action with respect to surrounding circumstances. Relativism is a concept that is teleological; it weighs right and wrong of an action with respect to culture and context. We have a heck of a discussion in some of my classes when I introduce the question "What does right and wrong have to do with legal and illegal?" Some of the logic people offer for their answer to this question can be scary.

I don't know if many of you are familiar with the Rick Warren "Purpose Driven Life" study, but one of the lessons stuck in my mind and I have introduced it to many people. He tells us about unreliable authorities in our lives that influence our decisions. Doctrine, the foundational concepts of a Christian life, whether aware or unaware, influences decisions we make. Warren tells us that we have others. One is culture (everyone else is doing it), another is tradition (this is how we have always done it), a third is reason (it seems logical), and last emotion (it feels like the right thing to do). (Warren, 2002) If you think about it, most of the decisions you have made have had one of these influences drive the outcome.

"Sir, my concern is not whether God is on our side: my greatest concern is to be on God's side, for God is always right." A. Lincoln

These very excuses are used every day in an effort to avoid the responsibility for doing the right thing. Absolutes do exist. God's word and His truth stand out. It doesn't matter if you are an atheist, agnostic, Protestant, Catholic, Muslim, or new age relativist, or whether you believe in situation ethics, existentialism, moral imperative, or eastern philosophies; the doctrine of God still applies. At the end, every knee will bend, and every head will bow. That is going to be a big surprise to some people.

In an age where truth is twisted, faith is slandered, and conviction is ridiculed we must have a good idea of who we believe, what we believe, and why we believe it. Our belief is that which defines our character and determines where we go, what we do, and what we are. We can't let our beliefs be molded by the vain and temporary whims of man, but instead on the foundations of God.

Truth combats error and light drives away darkness. We don't need to fight error as much as we need to seek and declare truth. Let's do some seeking…

"We made bad use of immortality, and so ended up dying; Christ made good use of mortality, so that we might end up living."

Augustine of Hippo, *Teaching Christianity: De Doctrina Christiana*

BASIC CHRISTIAN DOCTRINES

God the Son

Jesus himself asked "Who do you say the son of man is?" We start with this section of doctrine because how you answer this question is a measure of how you understand your faith.

Nearly anyone will tell you that Jesus lived, was a prophet, was a teacher, and maybe a miracle worker, but they may not believe what the Bible has to say about him.

There are a lot of arguments that can be made about the trinity, the existence of God, the Son, and the Spirit as one and the same. Unitarians believe as the Jews of the time did, that Jesus was "a man approved by God", as Peter described him, and would be the Messiah, the human king to come. Jews to this day are still looking for their deliverer. In order to understand the existence of Christ as the Son, as well as the Father, and the Holy Spirit we have been told that the trinity is "a mystery" and, as such, we cannot understand it.

In truth, I have struggled with this. There is no single sentence in the Bible that definitively states that Jesus is God. There is plenty of evidence supporting him as the Son of God, but not God himself. Our understanding of the trinity is built on a collection of explanations, not anyone defining statement. Yet, the doctrine of the Trinity and our understanding of Jesus as the Son of God is a central doctrine of our faith. We largely hinge our belief on John's description in his first chapter. He states that "In the beginning was the Word, and the Word was with God, and the Word was God. He was with God in the beginning. Through Him all things were made, without Him nothing as made that has been made." He adds "The Word became flesh and made His dwelling among us" (Chr1:14).

That description has always been good enough for me, but for those who delve into the archaic interpretations of the Bible greater definition is required. It seems, given the influence of Jewish law, the earliest Christians expected to see an earthly kingdom ruled by an earthly king in the form of a Messiah. It is natural to understand their hesitation about Jesus as the Son of God and even more so to claim He was a heretic. On the other side, the Gentiles were largely polytheistic, and it would have been easy for them to accept an explanation that there were three gods, so to speak.

Let's begin with two statements we can all agree on.

1. <u>God is the Creator of all life</u>

The first human created, Adam, was called a son of God

As God's first-born son Jesus was in Heaven before he came to earth

- "He is the image of the invisible God, the firstborn of all creation." (Colossians 1:15)
- "I have come down from heaven."—John 6:38; 8:23

2. <u>Jesus said he was the Son of God</u>
- the High Priest demanded of Jesus, "I charge you under oath by the living God: Tell us if you are the Christ, the Son of God" (Matthew 26:63). "'Yes, it is as you say,' Jesus replied.

The doctrine of sonship tells us that the second person of the trinity always existed as the Son, that there has always been a Father/Son relationship, and there has never been a time when he was not the Son of God.

- it was "the Son" who created all things, implying that he was the Son of God at creation (Colossians 1:13-16; Hebrews 1:2)
- there are many verses that speak of God sending the Son to earth to redeem sinful man (John 20:21; Galatians 4:4; 1 John 4:14; 1 John 4:10)

- "I came forth from the Father and have come into the world; I am leaving the world again, and going to the Father." John 16:28

The Son is the cornerstone in the foundation of Christianity – God's Son, John 3:16

"For God so loved the world that he gave his one and only Son, that whoever believes in him shall not perish but have eternal life."

So far, none of the statements we offer here are denied by the Latter-Day Saints, the Unitarians, or the Mormons. It seems as if most organized religions, aside from the Jews, are willing to accept the idea that Jesus was the Son of God. But we can't just leave it at that. We need to make the connection to the Trinity. After all, and a question I have always wondered about, if Jesus was God, why do the gospels record that He prayed to God?

So, are there three different ways of looking at God, three different roles God plays? Not really. The Bible indicates there are three distinct "persons" in the Father, Son, and Holy Spirit. Think of the language you read in the Bible. If the Father sent the Son, and the Son spoke to the Father, then there are those two distinct entities. Since the Son said He would send the Spirit into the world after He left there is a third, separate entity. At the beginning of this section, we mentioned that the Word was with God, so the very basic explanation is that there are two, not one. We begin to see that there are three "persons" not three different roles of God.

In trying to understand the Son we have to see that doctrine does not separate God into three parts. The Son is not one-third, the Father not one-third, or the Spirit not one-third. About the best explanation I have heard is that a man is, in essence, but as a person he is a father, a son, and husband…three beings existing at the same time, never separate, but always distinct. At no one time is the man only a father, or only a son, or only a husband; he is always all three.

Source: https://bible.knowing-jesus.com/topics/Jesus-Christ,-Son-Of-God

Q&A

1. Jesus often referred to himself as the Son of Man. He was the only begotten Son of God, so what did He mean? Is "son" a metaphor, not a reality?
2. Jesus offered several statements about His relation to God "I and the Father am one" (John10:30), "He who has seen me has seen the Father" (John14:9), "He who beholds Me beholds the One who sent Me."(John 12:45) How would these statements have helped those in His time understand His relationship with the Father? How do they help you understand it?

The Death of Christ

In his 1958 sermon *The Immutability of Christ* Charles Spurgeon said "There is one great event, which every day attracts more admiration than do the sun, and moon, and stars, when they march in their courses. That event is the death of our Lord Jesus Christ. To it, the eyes of all the saints who lived before the Christian era were always directed; and backwards, through the thousand years of history, the eyes of all modern saints are looking. Upon Christ, the angels in heaven perpetually gaze." (Spurgeon, 1958, Jan 3, New Park St. pulpit)

Christians believe that Jesus Christ died for their sins and that His death created a new covenant under His blood. Some people have asked if the death of Christ was really necessary. The bottom line, according to Paul, was that while we were still sinners Christ died for us. It is pretty clear that His death paid for our sins and offered redemption to us through grace. He was the last, and only, atoning sacrifice. He nailed death and sin to the cross, then left it behind.

There could be no Christianity without the death of Christ. He came to die for our sins. There is no Gospel, no salvation, no grace, no redemption without his death on the cross. This was foreshadowed in the Old Testament. The Passover symbolizes the shed blood of a lamb that saved believers from death. People in the Old Testament days understood the purpose of sacrifice. People in the New Testament based their faith on the vicarious sacrifice of Christ. His sacrifice both took our place as a substitute and paid the price for our sins.

That is not all though. His sacrifice was not an accident and he was not a martyr. His death was voluntary. It was also a victory over death and sin. The death of Jesus was significant because His death did not just cover sin, it redeemed sin. His physical death was important because of the resurrection that followed; however, it was not Jesus' physical death that paid the ransom for the sin of man. Jesus had taught, "The reason my Father loves me is that I lay down my life - only to take it up again. No one takes it from me, but I lay it down of my own accord. I have authority to lay it down and authority to take it up again. This command I received from my Father" John 10:17-18 The greatest commandment is to love one another. Such love extends to this sacrifice. When I was in college, we had the memorize the verse "Greater love has no man, than a man lay down his life for his friends." John 15:13 This is a picture of the level of love we should have for mankind, and the understanding we should have about the love that He has for us.

This brings us to five truths about the death of Christ.

When Jesus died, he died for the ungodly, for sinners, and for his enemies. Paul gets at how contrary this is to human nature when he writes, "For one will scarcely die for a righteous person, though perhaps for a good person one would dare to die, but God shows his love for us in that while we were sinners, Christ died for us" (Romans 5:7–8).

The death of Christ was effective in its purpose and its goal was not just to purchase the possibility of salvation, but a people for his own possession. "All that the Father gives to me will come to me, and whoever comes to me I will never cast out… And this is the will of him who sent me, that I should lose nothing of all that he has given me, but raise it up on the last day" (John 6:36, 39).

He died the death that we deserved. He bore the punishment that was justly ours. For everyone who believes in him, Christ took the wrath of God on their behalf. Peter writes, "[Jesus] himself bore our sin in his body on the tree that we might die to sin and live to righteousness. By his wounds you have been healed" (1 Peter 2:24).

His substitutionary death is the ultimate example of what love means, and Jesus calls those who follow him to walk in the same kind of life-laying-down love. John writes, "By this we know love, that he laid down his life for us, and we ought to lay down our lives for the brothers. But if anyone has the world's goods and sees his brother in need, yet closes his heart against him, how does God's love abide in him? Little children, let us not love in word or talk but in deed and in truth" (1 John 3:16).

Jesus's death enables us to have a joy-filled relationship with God, which is the highest good of the cross. Paul writes, "And you, who once were alienated and hostile in mind, doing evil deeds, he has now reconciled in his body of flesh by his death, in order to present you holy and blameless and above reproach before him" (Colossians 1:21–22).

Q&A

Jesus' last words on the cross are recorded as "Eli, Eli, lema sabachthani" (My God, my God, why have you abandoned me?). People have asked about this for years, but most don't know this was the beginning of a poem that Jesus would have known by heart. It was a poem of praise (Psalm22) and, in context, affirms His trust in God's will.

Here again we see women being specifically mentioned at the crucifixion of Christ. Women were direct witnesses to three major events in Christianity: his death, His burial, and His resurrection. Why do the gospel writers mention the women while largely minimalizing them during His ministry?

In the end, when so many had failed to see Christ for who he truly was, it was a Roman centurion who says, "this was truly the Son of God". What was going on at the time that would have caused him to come to this conclusion?

The Resurrection of Christ

The doctrine of the resurrection of Christ is one of the most critical elements of the foundation of Christianity. In Paul's teachings especially the resurrection is proclaimed.

First of all, we have to understand that Jesus was the first resurrected from a dead human body and returned to life in a new kind of body. Sure, we know about others who have been brought back to life by Elijah (1King 17;17), Elisha (2Kings 4;18), Elisha's body (2Kings 13:20), Jesus (Luke 8:49, John 11:1), Peter (Acts 9:36) but other than Jesus they were restored to bodies that would eventually die.

We should consider the chief effect his bodily death had and the way his resurrection influenced the spread of Christianity. He died, as a man, and the disciples were convinced he was dead. They fell apart. These weak men though, saw him again after such a final event and it emboldened them to confront those who persecuted them. They preached His return with everything to lose and, indeed, they did lose their lives for it.

Consider a tomb heavily guarded and sealed so His followers would not be able to steal the body. You have to know that the priests did everything they could to produce His body to prove He was dead. After all, his disciples all ran when he was arrested and would probably not risk their lives for a corpse. Lots of miracles took place during His ministry that the Sanhedrin tried to explain away, but His resurrection could not be denied. History shows us proof of His resurrection. Many people have tried to disprove the resurrection, but some very compelling evidence says otherwise.

Prof. Thomas Arnold, Oxford Chair of History — *"I have been used for many years to study the histories of other times, and to examine and weight the evidence of those who have written about them, and I know of no one fact in the history of mankind which is proved by better and fuller evidence of every sort, to the understanding of a fair inquirer, then the great sign which God hath given us that Christ died and rose again from the dead."(McDowell, 2017, p.191)*

Prof. Brooke Westcott, Cambridge - "Indeed, taking all the evidence together, it is not too much to say that there is no historic incident better or more variously supported than the resurrection of Christ. Nothing but the antecedent assumption that it must be false could have suggested the idea of deficiency in the proof of it." (McDowell, 2017, p.193)

Dr. Simon Greenleaf, Law Prof, Harvard - "It was therefore impossible that the apostles could have persisted in affirming the truths they had narrated, had not Jesus Christ actually risen from the dead, and had they not known the fact as certainly as they knew any other fact." (McDowell, 2017, p.195)

Several times Jesus declared He would rise from the dead

Mark 9.31; because he was teaching his disciples. He said to them, "The Son of Man is going to be delivered into the hands of men. They will kill him, and after three days he will rise."

Mark 10.34; "We are going up to Jerusalem," he said, "and the Son of Man will be delivered over to the chief priests and the teachers of the law. They will condemn him to death and will hand him over to the Gentiles, [34] who will mock him and spit on him, flog him and kill him. Three days later he will rise."

Luke 18.33; "they will flog him and kill him. On the third day he will rise again."

Paul told the Corinthians (15:3-5) "For I delivered to you as of first importance what I also received: that Christ died for our sins *in accordance with the Scriptures*, that he was buried, that he was raised on the third day *in accordance with the Scriptures*, and that he appeared to Cephas, then to the twelve." When he was referring to "according to the scriptures" he was thinking about Isaiah 53: 5,6 and its description of substitutionary atonement. "But he was pierced for our transgressions, he was crushed for our iniquities; the punishment that brought us peace was on him, and by his wounds we are healed. We all, like sheep, have gone astray, each of us has turned to our own way; and the LORD has laid on him the iniquity of us all." Paul was explaining that His death and resurrection was a fulfillment of the Old Testament narrative.

Furthermore, Jesus shared that righteousness would be imputed to us through His resurrection. Jesus explained to Martha, "Your brother will rise again." Martha said to Him, "I know that he will rise again in the resurrection on the last day." Jesus said to her, "I am the resurrection and the life; he who believes in Me will live even if he dies, and everyone who lives and believes in Me will never die. Do you believe this?" Jesus said to her, "Your brother will rise again" (John 11.23-26).

Romans 4:24; "...but also for us, to whom God will credit righteousness--for us who believe in him who raised Jesus our Lord from the dead."

Q&A

John presented three accounts of people who witnessed the resurrected Christ. Literally hundreds of people saw the resurrected Christ after His very public crucifixion. None of them ever expected to see him alive again and they all needed to be convinced that He was, indeed, alive again. All were convinced.

1. Mary went to the tomb but found it empty. She talked to someone she thought was the gardener, but then realized was Christ. What does the fact that the first person to see Him alive again was a woman do to confirm the reality of His resurrection? How does she respond to Him?
2. The disciples were hiding in a room locked away from the Jews. They had heard the message Mary told them about what she saw but could not believe without seeing for themselves. How does His appearance change their discouragement? Does His appearance help resolve discouragement in your life?
3. A disciple, Thomas, was not there when Jesus appeared to the others. How did he react to their news? Was his reaction unreasonable? Without seeing for yourself, what does it take for you to believe He was resurrected?

Salvation

Philippians tells us that salvation is a deliverance from suffering. To save is to deliver and it indicates victory over danger. The example from the Bible is Pauls' delivery from prison; he was saved. (Phil 1:9)

What we are addressing here is salvation of a spiritual nature. In Matthew we are told that being saved means going to heaven. (Matt 19:24). But what are we being saved from? I have always thought it meant being saved from myself, mostly. I am a sinful man born of a sinful nature. The consequence of my sin is death. Being saved, then, is the removal of that sin. It also means I have a home in heaven and share an inheritance with Jesus in the family of God. That was enough for me as a young man when I was saved. I confessed my sin to the body of the church, accepted Christ as my savior, and said I would live my life as close to His will as possible.

As a young man though, I did not fully comprehend the full nature of being saved, what it took to cover my sins, and what it meant to help others to be saved. I did not really have a very good handle on the concept of grace, the unmerited gift given to me in spite of myself. Now, as an older person, I have a better idea of just how much this should mean to me. Ephesians 2:8 ought to be ingrained in the heart of every Christian "…by grace ye are saved through faith, and that not of yourselves; it is the gift of God."

So, salvation is available through grace, a gift to sinners to reconcile them to their maker. Salvation must be the most extraordinary expression of grace. Then we see the definition of grace as a matter of faith. Faith exists in your mind and is generated through the influence of the Holy Spirit. No one can believe for you; you have to hear the word of God and come to know their meaning. Faith grows and can be strengthened. "Soundness of faith' comes through hearing, thinking, learning, and trusting, and sometimes by victory following rebuke." Titus 1:13

Now we have belief developing into faith, which allows me to be saved. Since the fall of man God has provided a way for us to be delivered from sin, meaning an eventual recovery from satan's influence. I think God is pleased when we study the word, become stronger believers, build our faith, and come to understand just what being saved means.

It's pretty simple if you just write it down. *"Believe on the Lord Jesus Christ and thou shalt be saved. "* (Acts 16:31) It wasn't so simple to make happen. What are we supposed to believe to be saved? There are a lot of versions out there on how to be saved. Satan has worked overtime to try and create this confusion. Here is the thesis statement for a study of salvation: Salvation is by grace through faith alone, not as a result of good works, so that God alone gets the glory. (Eph 2:8-10) The are five concepts here we have been building this explanation on 1) saved, 2) grace, 3) faith, 4) gift, and 5) glory.

I mentioned that there are numerous versions of how to be saved. Some people are still sold on the "works" doctrine, intimating that there must be some way to earn your way into heaven. Can you think of just one, of the many, verses in the Bible that contradicts this? I think of Luke 18 where the Pharisee was praying about all he had done to show his righteousness, and thanked God that he was not like the tax collector standing in the corner. The tax collector could not even look up to heaven as he asked for mercy for his sins. Jesus explained that the tax collector went home more justified than the Pharisee due to the genuine nature of his contrition. It isn't about works.

We all know Joel Olsteen or have probably heard his name. In a *60 Minutes* interview October 16th of 2007 he told the interviewer, Byron Pitts, that he has little gifting for teaching the word of God, instead opting rather to inspire and motivate people. He stated that what he preaches is closer to Dr. Phil or Oprah than Jesus or Paul. By his own admission he stays away from explaining theology or doctrine, explaining that there is scripture out there to back up what he says. Being saved isn't about feeling good about yourself because you are a good person.

Maybe it's about wanting to avoid the wrath of God. There is a doctrine about the wrath of God that isn't heard much anymore. It simply isn't anything people want to hear about. It's intolerant, it isn't acceptable, it too cruel. After all, where is the justice? The fact is, the concept of justice is what has been altered. If we ever got what we deserved, we would all be in trouble. Here again we fall on grace, the unmerited gift that helps us avoid the consequences of sin. Some things to keep in mind about God's wrath include 1) God's wrath is just, 2) God's wrath is to be feared, 3) God's wrath is consistent with both the Old and New testament, 4) God's wrath is his love in action against sin, and 5) God's wrath is satisfied in Christ. (Scheumann, 2014) As a kid in high school I was scared enough when I had to read "In the Hands of an Angry God" by Jonathan Edwards. When you read "But it is visibly clear that God is under no obligation to keep such a person from eternal destruction, not even for one moment. It doesn't matter how religious the man is or how many prayers he makes. Until he believes in Christ, God is not obligated in any way to protect him." and "Unconverted men walk over the pit of hell on a rotten covering." you pay attention. Maybe being saved is a little like being scared out of hell.

In the bigger picture though, I think that salvation is Gods way of allowing you to come home. I look at myself as a soul that has a body more than a body that has a soul. My soul has an eternal home. Our salvation gives all the glory to God and none to us. His will is that all should be saved. (1Tim 2:4) We see an invitation most Sundays when a sermon is delivered. We are being asked to believe, have faith, confess our sins, acknowledge Christ as our savior, and accept the gift of eternal life in heaven. The decision is personal, the gift is real, the love is eternal. I like this reason for salvation the most.

Q&A

1. Romans 10:13 says that "for whoever will call upon the name of the Lord will be saved." Does that mean that everyone who calls on His name will be saved?   It means that those who recognize His sovereignty over their souls will be saved. It is not just a statement; it is an understanding of His work through us.

2. When it comes to salvation, do we choose God, or does He choose us? Both, he chooses us for salvation, but we have to choose to accept it. Although we are chosen, we are enabled to choose Him. We are elected, are predestined, and have free will to pursue and accept our salvation.

John 15:16, "You did not choose Me, but I chose you...

Ephesians 1:4-5, "just as He chose us in Him before the foundation of the world, that we would be holy and blameless before Him...

2 Thess. 2:13...because God has chosen you from the beginning for salvation through sanctification by the Spirit and faith in the truth.

Baptism

To me the doctrine of baptism is about as simple to explain as they come...Jesus himself was baptized. Even though not a sinner and with no need to be cleansed of iniquity, he created a symbol of being buried and resurrected into a new life, as he would be. If we are to follow Jesus, we should be baptized in obedience as a public act of faith. After all, this is where the phrase "born again" is acted on.

Being born again comes from John 3: 1-21. "I tell you the truth, no one can see the kingdom of God unless he is born again." Jesus was explaining to a man, a Pharisee named Nicodemas, who wanted to know more about his teaching. Naturally, this was going to raise some questions from people who were very literally guessing the meaning of the statement. Jesus explained that a person must be born of water and the Spirit. The short answer is that sinners are spiritually dead in trespasses and sins but can receive spiritual life through faith in Christ. "And you He made alive, who were dead in trespasses and sins" (Eph 2:1) "Therefore, if anyone is in Christ, he is a new creation: the old has gone, the new has come!" (2 Corinthians 5:17). Jesus had explained to Nicodemus that the flesh gives birth to the flesh, but the Spirit gives birth to the Spirit.

Where did the idea of baptism come from? The origin of the word is Greek, *baptisma*, meaning to dip or dye and change the identification of something. An example would be white cloth dipped in blue dye which changes its identity down to its roots. Baptism was an old Jewish ritual, part of a ceremonial washing. A new priest was "baptized" into his new office to identify their new position. (Who is God, n.d.) When John the Baptist came around the idea of ceremonial cleansing was not new, and Jews came to him to confess their sins and be washed clean. This was not a baptism of salvation as we know it today because Christ had not yet died to pay for our sins. It was simply an act of repentance.

Keep this in mind about how the practice of baptism developed through Christianity and forward for Protestants. The church insisted, up to the Reformation, that infants were baptized into the body of the church. It was not a believer's baptism, not a choice. At that time there was no separation of power between church and state. For individuals to have a choice about baptism or take the Lord's Supper based on their own conviction, then it meant that the church would be a free and voluntary assembly. This would threaten the power of secular government. Believer's baptism was against the law since it threatened the law.

Something worthy of note here is that you never hear of Jesus baptizing anyone. In John 4: 1,2 it says that His disciples did the baptizing. Jesus presented himself as the Messiah. John claimed the superiority of Christ as the one who would baptize with the Holy Spirit, not water. He was not an imitator of John, but the one who would come to save mankind as the sacrifice for sin. This attaches the act of baptism to the fact of salvation. It establishes Christ superior to John, it offers a foundation for his disciples to baptize in his name, and it keeps anyone from claiming to be baptized by Jesus and, as such, superior to others. This allows every believer to be baptized in Christ instead of by Christ. It also means that sinners can still be saved and follow baptism after Christ went to heaven.

OK, but is baptism required to be saved? No, it is an act of obedience, following an example. After all, the criminal on the cross was promised paradise by Jesus and he was not baptized.

If baptism is a symbolic practice showing the public that the person dies to themselves, rises with Christ to a new life, and becomes a member of the family of God, then why are infants sometimes baptized? After all, surely, they could not know what it's all about. The explanation is that the child has no idea what is going on, but the parents want them baptized in order to become a member of the covenant, an old Jewish practice. It was a sacrament, a sign to the community of believers. Not until the 16th century did people begin to question infant baptism, the birth of Protestantism. The Pope was the head of the church until this time, and the church baptized infants "into the church". During the Protestant Reformation the basis for faith and salvation was placed squarely on the shoulders of the individual, not the practices of the church. As Protestants, our version of baptism is a personal, knowing, accountable act of obedience. We are not saved by rituals.

Q&A

1. I was baptized as a young child and probably did not fully understand the meaning of what I was doing. Should I be baptized again?
2. If you don't literally have to be baptized to be saved, then why do it?   Jesus was, it is an act of obedience, it follows the concept of being born again, it is a public confession

The Lord's Supper

There are two ordinances that Jesus mentioned for his church. One was baptism, the other was the Lord's Supper. In the early church this was called the eucharist, or "giving thanks" (Matt 26:27). In the catholic church it was called "mass", or "*missa est*", meaning "Go, it is discharged". Once upon a time, in the 16th century, during the Reformation, these ordinances were worth dying for. There are records from the time of the Catholic Queen Mary where protestants were beheaded for testifying that the body of Christ in the Lord's Supper was representative, what we call consubstantiation. People were also beheaded for taking part in believer's baptism. Prior to the Reformation, it was believed that the Lord's Supper was transubstantiation, actually believing the bread and wine were flesh and blood. For religions not Catholic, but closely related it was considered consubstantiation, wine, and bread "in the presence of" flesh and blood. For many of us though, it is representation, wine (juice) and bread in remembrance of the flesh and blood. After all, he said to "do this in remembrance of me".

There are several ways to look at how Paul explained the sacrament of the Lord's Supper. The most natural way to look at it is as a representation, that the bread represents the body of Christ. The Catholic catechism uses the word "represents" but adds a hyphen "re-presents", as if it is actually presenting again the body of Christ. (Piper, 2003) He goes on to explain the cup. When Christ said: "This cup is the new covenant in my blood." He did not mean the cup literally turned into a covenant. The cup, and the contents, "stand" for the new covenant. When Christ said: "I am the bread of life." He did not mean he turned into a loaf of bread. Even when Christ was trying to explain this to his followers, he could see that they were confused. He had to further explain that He was speaking figuratively, that the bread was his spirit and flesh is of no avail. Later in John 6:35 he stated: "I am the bread of life; whoever comes to me shall not hunger, and whoever believes in me shall not thirst." He was speaking spiritually again, that the body will surely need food and drink again, but the soul shall not want. In 1Cor 10:6 it refers to nourishing your heart on the blessings you have received

In the last section we saw where believer's baptism and taking the Lord's Supper as a matter of individual belief and conviction was against the law, heresy in the church. At the height of Catholic power, you took the wafer and wine as instructed with no regard for any personal connection to Christ. There was no personal reflection of faith. Anything else was an attack on church doctrine. This ties into this study. If we accept and allow governance of any religion to define our relationship to Christ then we diminish the sacrifice of the Lamb, we rob Him of His priesthood, we deny the true human-ness of Christ's nature. The sacrament of the Lord's Supper is a proclamation, a personal declaration of faith that is built on the spiritual risen and living Christ.

In light of our personal declaration of faith, let's review what is asked of us when we take part in the Supper. You have probably heard the pastor read "But let a man examine himself, and so let him eat of that bread, and drink of that cup" 1 Cor. 11:28 When we do this examining, what are we looking for?

First, we need to look within. Paul says this isn't about trying to determine whether we are worthy or not, because we aren't. It is about whether we are doing so in a worthy manner. Second, we ought to look backward as a memorial that reminds of His death on the cross. In my own imagination I have wondered how it would feel standing in the garden, knowing I was going to be betrayed, and allowing it to happen. Third, maybe we ought to look forward knowing that, as a member of the Lord's family, we can welcome the second coming. There are basically ten things to remember as we reflect on this sacrament.

1. The Lord's Supper is designed to elicit remembrance
2. The remembrance is commanded
3. The remembrance entails the use of tangible elements, bread and wine
4. It is a personal remembrance, not a corporate worship
5. There is also a personal reflection, a confession
6. In the remembering there is a proclamation of our Christianity
7. To partake we should remember that we are not worthy
8. This is not to be seen as just a meal; it is a sacrament
9. We are supposed to examine ourselves to understand our motives
10. This is an expression of God's grace and should not be missed

We live in a time where our practices have not been seriously challenged but are facing opposition. There has been a time when brutality was the hallmark of church doctrine. In our time, I am afraid that superficiality may be the hallmark of our church doctrine. We cannot get to the point where we lose connection with sound teaching based on solid Biblical truths.

Q&A

1. When Christ was giving the last supper, he said "This cup is the new covenant in my blood; do this, whenever you drink it, in remembrance of me." What is new about the "new covenant" He mentioned?

   Originally a Passover celebration for the Jews, now entry into a new covenant, including all people. Meaning moves from Passover to recognition of His sacrifice.

2. Taking part in the Supper is a very personal thing, and its meaning can be different for you at different points in your life. Which part of its meaning is most important for you at this point in your life?

The Fellowship of the Church

Literally, in Acts we see that those touched by the Gospel embraced the message and were baptized (Acts 2:41,42) More so though, we see an emphasis on fellowship, continued meeting, teaching, breaking of bread, fellowship, and prayer. In Hebrews it says, "Let us not neglect meeting together, as some have made a habit, but let us encourage one another, and all the more as you see the Day approaching."

In these verses of Acts we see development of the early church, the very earliest, primitive first days of the church. In its infancy they wanted to keep close to one another and keep communion, recognizing the strength it gave them (biblehub.com) There are stories where they sold their possessions, gave to the church, supported one another, and generally gave their lives to serving each other. We can probably all recall the tragic end Ananias and Sapphira met. In a time while most were giving all, they gave only a portion and fell dead when it was discovered. This isn't to say we are supposed to be doing the same, but the context allows us to get a feel for just how dedicated those early Christians were to be with each other, serve each other, and be strengthened through each other.

I grew up in Baptist churches where fellowship meant meeting in the Fellowship Hall for those infamous potluck dinners. Here we had dinner on the grounds, gravy in the grass, whatever you might call it…meals together that would allow a community of believers to talk about their work, their families, their concerns, and their church. To a young man this was a great time, but I wasn't really getting the idea about what "fellowship" really meant, just how deep it goes. Fellowship goes beyond occasional meetings; it is the fabric of a believer's society, the often unspoken values that form a bond between a congregation. I say "unspoken" because we rarely ever talk about our basic beliefs, the foundations of doctrine that tie us together.

We may be studying doctrine here because we are not talking about it elsewhere. The help one of our members needs may be found in a firmer understanding of what worship is and how a message applies to each of us. You might recall a time when you heard about a brother or sister in Christ who was struggling with something, perhaps even succumbed to it, and you never knew. Conditions like these are very private, but in small, often veiled ways people reach out to others for guidance. When our fellowship is strong, we know people well enough to hear what they are not saying and should open an opportunity that will allow them to share more if they are willing to.

It's hard to know when to be there for someone, but it isn't all that hard to be available, or at least willing. Most people will tell themselves that it is a pastoral staff job to field these needs, but I think we all know it is everyone's job. In small groups we offer time to ask for prayer for personal needs. I wonder how often though, a person in the group will call the other member later in the week and ask if they need help, or at least if things have improved.

It puts me in mind of those times when you casually ask someone how they are doing and get the usual response of "Great…how are you?" Do you ever wonder if we have become conditioned to say that to keep from actually getting further into the conversation? What would you do if someone actually said things weren't going so well right now and asked you to keep them in prayer about something? Most of us would be comfortable offering a hand of fellowship, a sounding board, or maybe a shoulder to lean on. Our fellowship is a matter of belonging to each other as brothers and sisters in Christ.

No discussion about fellowship would be honest without mentioning some negative issues that could come up. In Eph.5 we are told to avoid fellowship with the works of darkness. In 2Cor.6 we are asked how righteousness and iniquity, light and dark can share in the same fellowship. We have all heard that we will need to live *in* this world, but don't have to be *of* this world. There are several places in the Bible where fellowship should be withdrawn. Paul told Timothy that it is always wrong to share in the wickedness of others.

While we cannot avoid mingling with people of the world, we can be aware of their lingering influences on us. You can do one of two things here. You can withdraw from those people to the extent you can control, or you can decide if you are strong enough to avoid their influence and, instead, be a Christian influence on them. In the larger picture we are warned to be careful about formal associations with non-Christian groups because your argument may be seen as giving them credit for their beliefs. You don't have to get down in the dirt with them in order to make your point. Christians are very capable of opposing wickedness on their own. Consider planting the seed of righteousness and letting God take it from there. 2John 9:11 "Whosoever goeth onward and abideth not in the teaching of Christ, hath not God…if any one cometh unto you and bringeth not this teaching, receive him not into your house, and give him no greeting: for he that giveth him greeting partaketh in his evil works."

Before we leave the topic of contentious fellowship, we are obliged to touch on the fact that there may be negative fellowship issues inside our own body. I have never seen it done, but the Bible addresses the possibility of having to withdraw fellowship from a believer that is repeatedly unrepentant. I do hope to never have to witness that. 1John 2:19 "They went out from us, but they were not of us; for if they had been of us, they would have continued with us; but they went out that they might be made manifest that they all are not of us."

You will ask yourself three questions about fellowship 1) am I in the right fellowship with God, 2) do I demonstrate fellowship to my fellow believers, and 3) do I know how to extend fellowship to non-believers and not weaken my own testimony? From what I read in the Bible, fellowship is like a triangle. When the bonds between God, myself, and my brother are unbroken then true fellowship exponentially strengthens us all. We don't create the basis of fellowship ourselves. Human authority is inadequate, changing, and contradictory. Fellowship is not determined by our emotions, personal likes, or traditional standards. Fellowship erases barriers and is not measured or tempered by the concepts of "liberty" or "relevance". It doesn't make any difference what one man desires or what culture demands; fellowship is formed in the teachings of Christ. Faith and fellowship cannot be separated. There must be unity of faith to maintain a bond of peace with one another.

Q&A

1. Have you ever experienced hurt within the community of your congregation? If so, does it cause you to struggle with the community even now, or did the experience help you grow and mature in your walk with God?
2. There can be many differences between people and people groups in a church community. How does the gospel unite us at a deeper level than differences that would normally divide us?
3. Are there areas of your life where you are more inclined to think in terms of "I" instead of "we" as a member of the church body when it comes to major life decisions (parenting, dating, marriage, aspirations)?

Mission of the Church

Apparently, there are several parts to the mission of the church. I have heard it explained that the church was created by God, belongs to Christ and energized by the Holy Spirit. I needed a definition of the church before I could understand its mission. For a definition of what the church is, I leaned on Focus on the Family, a global Christian ministry we have probably all heard of.

The whole area of study surrounding "the church" is called ecclesiology, a general term referring to gathering or assembling of believers. If we look at the beginnings of the church, we know that it was not a building, but the fellowship, ministry, and worship conducted by people. Beyond that, we have the visible church, the buildings we see, and we have the invisible church, people united in Christ. The church is fallible though, as people are not perfect, and buildings fall apart. That's alright though, because the body of believers, corporately, is stronger when they come together. Together believers worship, edify, and evangelize. In other words, they express their love of the Creator, they nurture and support one another, and they reach out to share the good news of the gospel to nonbelievers. The church faces challenges in fulfilling these roles but perseveres. As C.S. Lewis shared, "In spite of all the unfortunate differences between Christians, what they agree on is still something pretty big and pretty solid: big enough to blow any of us sky-high if it happens to be true. And if it's true, it's quite ridiculous to put off doing anything about it simply because Christians don't fully agree among themselves." (Hooper, 1996)

This helps explain what the mission of the church is then. It is to glorify Christ (Eph 1:11-12), to build up the saints (2Cor 12:25), and to make disciples (Matt 28: 19-20). As W. C. Robinson says in *Baker's Dictionary of Theology*, "Our Lord Jesus Christ is the sun about which the whole mission of the church revolves. Public worship is the encounter of the risen Redeemer with His people; evangelism is calling men to the Savior; publishing the law of God is proclaiming His lordship; Christian nurture is feeding His lambs and disciplining His flock; ministering to the needs of men is continuing the work of the Great Physician." (Harrison, et.al 1987)

I get this mind picture when I think about the mission of the church revolving around Christ, like planets around the sun. The idea came to me that we have two dynamics working here, one centrifugal, the other centripetal. We expand our faith to send the word out and, in turn, mission outreach draws people in. We have an expanding universe of faith, and people are drawn (gravity) to the message. There is a design here, a purpose, a reason why the mission of the church exists. Every purpose comes with a design, a specific form for its mission. A knife is meant to cut; a spoon does something different than a fork. *The purpose determines the form; the shape determines its function.* Applying that to our discussion here, we conclude that our mission was not made for the church, but the church was made for the mission, God's mission.

In many cases, this seems to be done backwards. God doesn't so much have a mission for His church in the world as He has a church for his mission in the world. In short, He had a mission, *then* He had a church. The church exists for His mission. If you and I are the church, then we have a mission. We are saved, but what are we saved for? We are saved to bring glory to Christ by speaking His word (evangelism), talking about what He cares about (truth), and living in ways that reflect Him (love). We are saved for His mission, to care for each other and bring others to Him. As with the knife, the fork, and the spoon, this is the purpose, the mission, of the church.

Q&A

1. Who, exactly, is a minister, and what are they supposed to do in the church?

    If we look at the New Testament, we know that Christ came not to receive service, but to offer it. "Ministry" simply means service. Of course, it has developed into a more vocational role over the years. We have a pastor, and the church has a staff, all people who work for the church to keep it running. But we are ministers ourselves. We are called to serve. Every Christian should be in the ministry of serving others. That isn't limited to spiritual things; it also means practical things.

2. Does the mission of the church mean getting involved in social issues and causes?

    I see two ways to look at this. You have your aggressive activists who picket abortion clinics, write to government representatives, and campaign for conservative candidates, then you have the "I am not of this world" school of thought, the people who refuse to get involved in the culture of the world. The Bible tells us to be good citizens, to live by the law.

Jesus did not come to change the governments of the world, but create a new spiritual order. If we live by His example, we don't indulge ourselves in the notion that we should change the world by demanding things be done "the right way". Instead, we live according to the Word and change the hearts of man who, in turn, may change the culture of mankind. It's not our job to clean up the culture as much as it is to keep our small part of it clean, not as holier than thou, but as a light in darkness.

The picture of the Christian in the world is well illustrated by the analogy of the train station. We (Christians) are waiting in the station to board the northbound (heavenly) train. We are surrounded by people who are preparing to board the southbound train, completely unaware of its tragic destination. Should we spend our time and energy pleading with them to switch trains? Or do we merely tidy up the train station instead? The answer is obvious, and those who would tidy up the culture for the culture's sake are not only missing the point, but they are also misunderstanding the reason God leaves us in the world—to be His witness to the lost and condemned. Such a mission is far more "good and profitable to men" (Titus 3:8) than any amount of social or political activism. (got questions.org)

3. Why are there different Christian denominations?

The fact that denominations exist is a product of division in the church. These divisions have historically linked back to the Reformation, where Protestants separated from the Roman Catholic church, loosely formed as Lutherans, Reformed Catholics, Anabaptists, and Anglican. Even in these divisions there are differences, largely in form, usually not in doctrine. A Presbyterian church in Uganda may worship differently than one in Texas, but their core beliefs would be the same.

There are two main problems with denominations. The first is that there is nowhere in scripture that calls for different denominations. The call is for unity. This points out the second problem, that denominations are the result of separation. These differences can be over interpretations of scripture, interpretations of sacraments, self-interests, and personal agendas. The media picks up on this today and uses it to further separate us, emphasizing that we are not cohesive in our beliefs.

CONCLUSION

As mentioned early in this study, we are living in, and may have been for some time, an era described in 1Tim 4" ...some shall depart from the faith, giving heed to seducing spirits and doctrines of evil". We won't know if we are departing from the faith unless we understand our basic doctrines.

"I want God, not my idea of God." --C.S. Lewis

Usually, when we see a sign that says "Danger" or "Beware" we take notice and avoid the problem. The problem here is that we often think we are smarter than we are, we know how to interpret the Bible, and we are confident that the lessons of the Bible might be out of touch, or not really applicable to modern times. John hung out such a danger sign "Whosoever transgresseth, and abideth not in the doctrine of Christ, hath not God. He that abideth in the doctrine of Christ, he hath both the Father and the Son" (2 Jn. 9).

His warning was largely ignored, and now we have divisions in His church due to the logic of man, the reasoning of man, and the pride of man. The church is facing a crisis, as it always seems to. Paul warned the Corinthians about their wayward practices. The early churches and those of the middle ages lead us up to the Reformation, an attempt to set things right that ended up splitting believers into many forms of religion. Today Christians are being persecuted openly by Islam and subtly diminished by our own government. It is a spiritual battle, but one we know is already won.

Although the church may be in continual crisis, it has a constant stability. The world is introducing inclinations and proclivities into our churches and we have to know it when we see it if we are going to negotiate current cultural contexts. Four themes exist that we should know about as we bring this study to a close.

- We are in an age where people are completely consumed by expressive individualism. People define their existence in terms of their personal identities. Concepts of liberty and rights are misconstrued as a license to live for yourself.

Remember that we do not belong to ourselves; we are heirs of His kingdom, bought with blood.

- In a society that relegates faith to the private world of self we have to be sensible about our view of religion and faith. Science should not be the judge of public morality and identity. Our faith does belong to us as individuals, but as a church. We should not define good, moral, and godly in terms of what is rewarding and pragmatic. Sometimes the right thing to do is very uncomfortable.

- Not only are people seeing Christianity as old fashioned, but it is also being criticized as dangerous. The moral revolution we are living in sees our doctrine as a threat, a problem, an extreme belief. What was once celebrated as the soul of this country is being marginalized.

- Even in this age of increased connectivity (the internet) we are increasingly disconnected, fragmented, and polarized. People distrust institutions more now, there is less solidarity, less identification as a nation, and more insulation between government and the governed. The challenge we face is to resist changing our worship into a place for mutual fulfillment. We don't come to church to self-actualize, to self-identify, to self- anything…we come together to glorify God. (Wax, 2018)

There are certain basic doctrines we should believe, beyond which there may be room for different styles of worship. This is one of the reasons we study doctrine, to know when are about to step onto the slippery slope of manmade reasoning, to slide into self-affirmation. We study doctrine not for the sake of doctrine itself, but for its application and the love of God's word for us.

We study doctrine because it leads to love; to know God equips you to act in love. We study doctrine because it leads to humility; it reveals the distance between His holiness and our sinfulness. We study doctrine because it leads to obedience; we pursue Him and not cold facts. We study doctrine because it leads to unity; it draws a clear connection between spiritual growth and the unity of believers. We study doctrine because it leads to worship; we are lifted in amazement at the sheer power and glory of God. We study doctrine because it leads to safety; understanding its instruction keeps us from wandering and helps us recognize false words. (challis.com, 2014)

REFERENCES

Bible Hub Commentary, Acts 2:42. Retrieved May 30, 2019 from
https://biblehub.com/acts/2-42.htm

Bloom, P. (Nov. 2015) "Scientific Faith is Different From Religious
Faith". The Atlantic (Science). Retrieved Apr. 12, 2020
https://www.theatlantic.com/science/archive/2015/11/why
-scientific-faith-isnt-the-same-as-religious-faith/417357/

Challis.com (2014) "Six reasons to study doctrine". Retrieved June 7,
2019 from https://www.challies.com/articles/6-great-
reasons-to-study-doctrine/

Conner, Kevin (1995) The Foundations of Christian Doctrine, City
Christian Publishing, Portland, OR.

Edwards, J. (1741) "Sinners in the Hands of an Angry God: A
Sermon Preached at Enfield, Connecticut", July 8

Gilbert, Travis (2014) Borrowed from Joshua Harris' book *Dug Down
Deep*, p. 16

Goldberg, G.J. (1995) "The Coincidences of the Testimonium of
Josephus and the Emmaus Narrative of Luke" The Journal
for the Study of the Pseudepigrapha 13 (1995) pp. 59-77.

Guardian of Truth (1983) 27, 20, p. 615 Retrieved June14, 2019 from
https://www.google.com/search?ei=TNMrXZjPLMq3tAaR
2YXoCw&q=guardian+of+truth+XXVII&oq=guardian+of
+truth+XXVII&gs_l=psy-
ab.3..33i160.182591.194456..196465...6.0..0.171.1544.2j10......0
....1..gws-wiz.......0i71j0j0i22i30j33i22i29i30.pGrLheHQ4Ms

Gotquestions.org "Should the Church get involved" Retrieved
June08, 2019 from https://www.gotquestions.org/church-
social.html

Harrison, E., Bromiley, G. & Henry, C. (1987) Bakers Dictionary of

Theology Baker Publishing Group, Grand Rapids, MI

Hooper, W. (1996) C.S. Lewis: Companion & Guide (Harper, San Francisco) excerpted from C.S. Lewis BBC radio talk, p. 307

Lennox, J. (2018) Determined to Believe: The Sovereignty of God, Freedom, Faith, and Human Responsibility (Zondervan Publishing)

Mataxas, E. (2016) If You Can Keep It: The forgotten promise of American liberty (Penguin, New York)

McDowell, J. (2017) "Evidence That Demands a Verdict: Life Changing Truth for a Skeptical World" Thomas Nelson publishing, Nashville, TN

Metaxas, Eric (2014) "Science Increasingly Makes the Case for God" Dec.25 Wall Street Journal

http://ericmetaxas.com/media/articles/science-increasingly-makes-case-god/

Piper, J. (2003) "Why We Eat the Lord's Supper" Retrieved Apr. 1, 2019   https://www.desiringgod.org/messages/why-we-eat-the-lords-supper-part-1

Pitts, B. (2007) *The Paul Edwards Program,*" *WLQV Detroit*, October 23, 2007

Scheumann, J. (2014) "Five Truths About the Wrath of God", Retrieved Mar. 29, 2019 https://www.desiringgod.org/articles/five-truths-about-the-wrath-of-god

Reagan, D. (2018) "Applying the Science of Probability to the Scriptures"

http://christinprophecy.org/articles/applying-the-science-of-probability-to-the-scriptures/

Saad, L. (May 2017) "Record Few Americans Believe Bible Is Literal

Word of God", Gallup Poll Social Series, Social and Policy Issues, Retrieved Apr 14, 2020 https://news.gallup.com/poll/210704/record-few-americans-believe-bible-literal-word-god.aspx

Spurgeon, C. (1958) "Sermons From the Park Street Pulpit", The *Immutability of Christ*, Retrieved Mar.4, 2019, https://www.spurgeon.org/resource-library/sermons/context/new-park-street-pulpit

Vatican News (2019) *Pope Francis: Christian Unity is not Optional*, Retrieved May, 2019 https://www.vaticannews.va/en/pope/news/2019-01/pope-francis-christian-unity-general-audience-appeal.html

Velarde, Robert (2009) "How Do We Know the Bible is True?" https://www.focusonthefamily.com/faith/the-study-of-god/how-do-we-know-the-bible-is-true/how-do-we-know-bible-is-true

Warren, R. (2002) "The Purpose Driven Life", Zondervan, Grand Rapids, MI

Wax, T. (2018) "Four Challenges Facing the Church in the West Today" Retrieved June 16, 2019 from https://www.thegospelcoalition.org/blogs/trevin-wax/4-big-challenges-facing-church-west-today/

"Who is God?" (n.d.). Retrieved Mar 29, 2019, from https://www.allaboutgod.com/who-is-god.htm.

Witt, J. (2007) "Does George Smoot, Nobel Laureate, see evidence of design in the cosmos?" https://evolutionnews.org/2007/02/does_george_smoot_nobel_laurea/

APPENDIX

135 PROPHESIES MET IN THE FIRST 35 CHAPTERS OF DANIEL

PROPHECIES FULFILLED BY JESUS CHRIST

Although this list is not exhaustive, you'll find 44 messianic predictions clearly fulfilled in Jesus Christ, along with supporting references from the Old and New Testament.

44 Messianic Prophecies Fulfilled by Jesus Christ

	Prophecies About Jesus	Old Testament Scripture	New Testament Fulfillment
1	Messiah would be born of a woman.	Genesis 3:15	Matthew 1:20 Galatians 4:4
2	Messiah would be born in Bethlehem.	Micah 5:2	Matthew 2:1 Luke 2:4-6
3	Messiah would be born of a virgin.	Isaiah 7:14	Matthew 1:22-23 Luke 1:26-31
4	Messiah would come from the line of Abraham.	Genesis 12:3 Genesis 22:18	Matthew 1:1 Romans 9:5
5	Messiah would be a descendant of Isaac.	Genesis 17:19 Genesis 21:12	Luke 3:34
6	Messiah would be a descendant of Jacob.	Numbers 24:17	Matthew 1:2
7	Messiah would come from the tribe of Judah.	Genesis 49:10	Luke 3:33 Hebrews 7:14
8	Messiah would be heir to King David's throne.	2 Samuel 7:12-13 Isaiah 9:7	Luke 1:32-33 Romans 1:3
9	Messiah's throne will be anointed and eternal.	Psalm 45:6-7 Daniel 2:44	Luke 1:33 Hebrews 1:8-12
10	Messiah would be called Immanuel.	Isaiah 7:14	Matthew 1:23
11	Messiah would spend a season	Hosea 11:1	Matthew 2:14-15

	in Egypt.		
12	A massacre of children would happen at Messiah's birthplace.	Jeremiah 31:15	Matthew 2:16-18
13	A messenger would prepare the way for Messiah	Isaiah 40:3-5	Luke 3:3-6
14	Messiah would be rejected by his own people.	Psalm 69:8 Isaiah 53:3	John 1:11 John 7:5
15	Messiah would be a prophet.	Deuteronomy 18:15	Acts 3:20-22
16	Messiah would be preceded by Elijah.	Malachi 4:5-6	Matthew 11:13-14
17	Messiah would be declared the Son of God.	Psalm 2:7	Matthew 3:16-17
18	Messiah would be called a Nazarene.	Isaiah 11:1	Matthew 2:23
19	Messiah would bring light to Galilee.	Isaiah 9:1-2	Matthew 4:13-16
20	Messiah would speak in parables.	Psalm 78:2-4 Isaiah 6:9-10	Matthew 13:10-15, 34-35
21	Messiah would be sent to heal the brokenhearted.	Isaiah 61:1-2	Luke 4:18-19
22	Messiah would be a priest after the order of Melchizedek.	Psalm 110:4	Hebrews 5:5-6
23	Messiah would be called King.	Psalm 2:6 Zechariah 9:9	Matthew 27:37 Mark 11:7-11
24	Messiah would be praised by little children.	Psalm 8:2	Matthew 21:16
25	Messiah would be betrayed.	Psalm 41:9 Zechariah 11:12-13	Luke 22:47-48 Matthew 26:14-16
26	Messiah's price money would be used to buy a potter's field.	Zechariah 11:12-13	Matthew 27:9-10
27	Messiah would be falsely accused.	Psalm 35:11	Mark 14:57-58
28	Messiah would be silent before his accusers.	Isaiah 53:7	Mark 15:4-5
29	Messiah would be spat upon and	Isaiah 50:6	Matthew 26:67

	struck.		
30	Messiah would be hated without cause.	Psalm 35:19 Psalm 69:4	John 15:24-25
31	Messiah would be crucified with criminals.	Isaiah 53:12	Matthew 27:38 Mark 15:27-28
32	Messiah would be given vinegar to drink.	Psalm 69:21	Matthew 27:34 John 19:28-30
33	Messiah's hands and feet would be pierced.	Psalm 22:16 Zechariah 12:10	John 20:25-27
34	Messiah would be mocked and ridiculed.	Psalm 22:7-8	Luke 23:35
35	Soldiers would gamble for Messiah's garments.	Psalm 22:18	Luke 23:34 Matthew 27:35-36
36	Messiah's bones would not be broken.	Exodus 12:46 Psalm 34:20	John 19:33-36
37	Messiah would be forsaken by God.	Psalm 22:1	Matthew 27:46
38	Messiah would pray for his enemies.	Psalm 109:4	Luke 23:34
39	Soldiers would pierce Messiah's side.	Zechariah 12:10	John 19:34
40	Messiah would be buried with the rich.	Isaiah 53:9	Matthew 27:57-60
41	Messiah would resurrect from the dead.	Psalm 16:10 Psalm 49:15	Matthew 28:2-7 Acts 2:22-32
42	Messiah would ascend to heaven.	Psalm 24:7-10	Mark 16:19 Luke 24:51
43	Messiah would be seated at God's right hand.	Psalm 68:18 Psalm 110:1	Mark 16:19 Matthew 22:44
44	Messiah would be a sacrifice for sin.	Isaiah 53:5-12	Romans 5:6-8

Sources: *100 Prophecies Fulfilled by Jesus: Messianic Prophecies Made Before the Birth of Christ* y Rose Publishing; *Book of Bible Lists* by H.L. Willmington; NKJV Study Bible; Life Application Study Bible.

Workbook

The following is intended to be used as a sort of study workbook. You can divide these into weeks, sessions, or however you care to use the study. The Introduction served as a first lesson, then each doctrine could serve as another lesson. You could combine two or three doctrines per lesson. You will be surprised at the questions and comments these doctrines will bring up when you get a group together to discuss them.

Introduction - Why study doctrine?

Culture and religion – why you believe what you do

____
____
____
____
____
____

"For the time will come when people will not put up with sound doctrine. Instead, to suit their own desires, they will gather around them a great number of teachers to say what their itching ears want to hear." 1 Tim

 The apostate church, fallen from original authority 1) man created doctrine, 2) church created doctrine

____
____
____
____
____
____

You know you have gone blind when you can see nothing wrong with something that God has called sin.

We have to have a working knowledge of sound doctrine to both <u>defend ourselves</u> and our families from the arguments of others and to <u>clearly offer our faith</u> to others as a way of salvation. A single person is poorly qualified to expertly interpret and expound on the details of theology.

Our salvation is directly related to what Christ accomplished on the cross, what he secured by His resurrection, and what He is doing in our lives through the Holy Spirit

____

____

____

____

____

Guiding precepts

Our theology is strong if scriptural teaching is reflected in how we live with one another. This study will take a closer look at the deity of God, the life, death and resurrection of Christ, and the salvation it offers us. Then we will take a look at what the church is and what it is supposed to be doing. Let me offer you a topic sentence, a guiding precept, for each area we intend to study.

<u>God the Son</u> - We believe that Christ is 100% God and 100% man. He exists in three persons - Father, Son, and Holy Spirit - each being a distinct person with a distinct function but all of one essence and all possessing the same nature, perfection, and attributes.

<u>The Death of Christ</u> – We believe that the Son of Man was born to die in order to save sinners. He willingly offered himself as a sacrifice to pay sin's price that we might be presented to the Father without blame.

<u>The Resurrection of Christ</u> - We hold that Christ was buried, then literally and bodily resurrected three days later.

<u>Salvation</u> – All men are born sinful but may be brought from death to eternal life repentant of sin believing that Christ is their Lord and savior.

<u>Baptism</u> – Baptism is an ordinance, an act of obedience symbolizing the death, burial, and resurrection of Christ. In itself, it does not cleanse, purify, or otherwise save.

<u>The Lord's Supper</u> - This is the other ordinance we are asked to obey. Whereas baptism is done once, this is a repeated act of individual reflection to symbolize the sacrifice made on our behalf.

<u>The Church</u> – This is the organized body of believers brought together under a common faith and fellowship as the body of Christ on earth.

<u>The Church's Mission</u> – We have a responsibility to win, baptize, and teach all things to "the nations" commanded of the Lord. This is a basic commission given to all believers.

Context

The Bible - God gave His word to his people as the only authoritative standard for their faith and life.

____
____
____
____
____
____

Science - Since the Enlightenment scientists have sought a natural, rather than supernatural, explanation of life and creation.

____
____
____
____
____
____

Instead of the Bible being outdated by science, we find that science is actually confirming ancient accounts of our origins.

Oxford professor of mathematics, Dr. John Lennox summarizes the impact of these findings. *"The more we get to know about our universe, the more the hypothesis that there is a Creator . . . gains in credibility as the best explanation of why we are here."*

I can merely present you with some topics based on sound theology and offer a forum of reflection. Paul told Timothy to "Take heed to thyself and unto doctrine; continue in them. In doing so you will save yourself and them that hear thee." 1Tim 4:16 If there is going to be a theme for this study, this might be a good one.

Arguments against, and the need for, doctrine

There are any number of arguments out there that are used to undermine solid Christian doctrine.

Universalism

____

____

New Age Movement

____

____

Legalism

____

____

Hyper grace

____

____

The Emerging church

____

____

Behind all these false ideologies is the belief that Scripture is not infallible, and truth simply changes with the times. A 2014 Gallup poll revealed that:

- 22 percent of Americans believe the Bible is the actual Word of God and should be taken literally
- 28 percent believe it is the actual Word of God, but with multiple possible interpretations
- 28 percent believe the Bible is the inspired Word of God but should not be taken literally
- 18 percent believe it is an ancient book of legends, history and moral precepts written by man

We aren't called to be like other Christians; we are called to be like Christ.

Objections to the need for doctrine - Today there is a movement to turn away from the sound doctrines of the Word and cling to the philosophies of men.

____

____

____

____

____

____

____

Need for Doctrine - We live in a world of relativism. Many people will tell you right and wrong depend on the situation and that there are no absolutes.

____

____

____

____

____

____

____

Application

We are living in, and may have been for some time, an era described in 1Tim 4 "…some shall depart from the faith, giving heed to seducing spirits and doctrines of evil". We won't know if we are departing from the faith unless we understand our basic doctrines.

The world is introducing inclinations and proclivities into our churches and we have to know it when we see it if we are going to negotiate current cultural contexts.

There are certain basic doctrines we should believe, beyond which there may be room for different styles of worship. This is one of the reasons we study doctrine, to know when are about to step onto the slippery slope of manmade reasoning, to slide into self-affirmation. We study doctrine not for the sake of doctrine itself, but for its application and the love of God's word for us.

"Those who teach by their doctrine must teach by their life, or else they pull down with one hand what they build up with the other."

Matthew Henry

A Review of Basic Christian doctrines

God the Son

Jesus himself asked "Who do you say the son of man is?" We start with this section of doctrine because how you answer this question is a measure of how you understand your faith.

Nearly anyone will tell you that Jesus lived, was a prophet, was a teacher, and maybe a miracle worker, but they may not believe what the Bible has to say about him.

Can you find a single sentence in the Bible that definitively states that Jesus is God?

Two statements we can all agree on:

God is the Creator of all life

Jesus said he was the Son of God

We need to make the connection to the Trinity. After all, and a question I have always wondered about, if Jesus was God, why do the gospels record that He prayed to God?

So, are there three different ways of looking at God, three different roles God plays?

The Death of Christ

There could be no Christianity without the death of Christ. He came to die for our sins. There is no Gospel, no salvation, no grace, no redemption without his death on the cross.

The death of Jesus was significant because His death did not just cover sin, it redeemed sin. His physical death was important because of the resurrection that followed; it was not Jesus' physical death that paid the ransom for the sin of man.

This brings us to five truths about the death of Christ.

When Jesus died, he died for the ungodly, for sinners, and for his enemies. The death of Christ was effective in its purpose and its goal was not just to purchase the possibility of salvation, but a people for his own possession. He died the death that we deserved. He bore the punishment that was justly ours. For everyone who believes in him, Christ took the wrath of God on their behalf.

His substitutionary death is the ultimate example of what love means, and Jesus calls those who follow him to walk in the same kind of life-laying-down love. Jesus's death enables us to have a joy-filled relationship with God, which is the highest good of the cross.

The Resurrection of Christ

The doctrine of the resurrection of Christ is one of the most critical elements of the foundation of Christianity.

It is critical to understand that Jesus was the first resurrected from a dead human body and returned to life in a new kind of body.

Many people have tried to disprove the resurrection, but some very compelling evidence says otherwise.

Paul told the Corinthians (15:3-5) "For I delivered to you as of first importance what I also received: that Christ died for our sins *in accordance with the Scriptures*, that he was buried, that he was raised on the third day *in accordance with the Scriptures*, and that he appeared to Cephas, then to the twelve."   When he was referring to "according to the scriptures" he was thinking about Isaiah 53: 5,6 and its description of substitutionary atonement.

Salvation

Philippians tells us that salvation is a deliverance from suffering. To save is to deliver and it indicates victory over danger. What we are addressing here is salvation of a spiritual nature.

In Matthew we are told that being saved means going to heaven. (Matt 19:24). But what are we being saved from?

It's pretty simple if you just write it down. *"Believe on the Lord Jesus Christ and thou shalt be saved. "* (Acts 16:31) **It wasn't so simple to make happen.**

Baptism

Even though not a sinner and with no need to be cleansed of iniquity, Jesus created a symbol of being buried and resurrected into a new life, as he would be.

Baptism, in history, and act of repentance. It was not a believer's baptism, not a choice.

You never hear of Jesus baptizing anyone. John claimed the superiority of Christ as the one who would baptize with the Holy Spirit, not water. This attaches the act of baptism to the fact of salvation.

This allows every believer to be baptized in Christ instead of by Christ.

The Lord's Supper

Up until the time of the Reformation it was believed that the Lord's Supper was transubstantiation, actually believing the bread and wine were flesh and blood.

For many of us though, it is representation, wine (juice) and bread in remembrance of the flesh and blood. After all, he said to "do this in remembrance of me".

If we accept and allow governance of any religion to define our relationship to Christ then we diminish the sacrifice of the Lamb, we rob Him of His priesthood, we deny the true human-ness of Christ's nature. The sacrament of the Lord's Supper is a proclamation, a personal declaration of faith that is built on the spiritual risen and living Christ.

"But let a man examine himself, and so let him eat of that bread, and drink of that cup" 1 Cor. 11:28 When we do this examining, what are we looking for?

The Fellowship of the Church

In Hebrews it says, "Let us not neglect meeting together, as some have made a habit, but let us encourage one another, and all the more as you see the Day approaching."

Fellowship goes beyond occasional meetings; it is the fabric of a believer's society, the often-unspoken values that forms a bond between a congregation.

When our fellowship is strong, we know people well enough to hear what they are not saying and should open an opportunity that will allow them to share more if they are willing to.

In Eph.5 we are told to avoid fellowship with the works of darkness. In 2Cor.6 we are asked how righteousness and iniquity, light and dark can share in the same fellowship. We have all heard that we will need to live *in* this world, but don't have to be *of* this world. While we cannot avoid mingling with people of the world, but we can be aware of their lingering influences on us.

You can do one of two things here. 1) You can withdraw from those people to the extent you can control. 2) you can decide if you are strong enough to avoid their influence and, instead, be a Christian influence on them.

There may be negative fellowship issues inside our own body. the Bible addresses the possibility of having to withdraw fellowship from a believer that is repeatedly unrepentant. 1John 2:19 "They went out from us, but they were not of us; for if they had been of us, they would have continued with us; but they went out that they might be made manifest that they all are not of us."

Three questions about fellowship

1) am I in the right fellowship with God,

2) do I demonstrate fellowship to my fellow believers, and

3) do I know how to extend fellowship to non-believers and not weaken my own testimony?

It doesn't make any difference what one man desires or what culture demands; fellowship is formed in the teachings of Christ. Faith and fellowship cannot be separated. There must be unity of faith to maintain a bond of peace with one another.

The Church's Mission

The whole area of study surrounding "the church" is called ecclesiology, a general term referring to gathering or assembling of believers. If we look at the beginnings of the church, we know that it was not a building, but the fellowship, ministry, and worship conducted by people.

Together believers worship, edify, and evangelize. In other words, they express their love of the Creator, they nurture and support one another, and they reach out to share the good news of the gospel to nonbelievers. The church faces challenges in fulfilling these roles

The mission of the church is to glorify Christ (Eph 1:11-12), to build up the saints 2 Cor 12:25, and to make disciples (Matt 28: 19-20).

As W. C. Robinson says in *Baker's Dictionary of Theology*, "Our Lord Jesus Christ is the sun about which the whole mission of the church revolves. (Harrison, et.al 1987)

A mind picture about the mission of the church revolving around Christ, like planets around the sun. The idea came to me that we have two dynamics working here, one centrifugal, the other centripetal. We expand our faith to send the word out and, in turn, mission outreach draws people in.

We conclude that our mission was not made for the church, but the church was made for the mission, God's mission. God doesn't so much have a mission for His church in the world as He has a church for his mission in the world. In short, He had a mission, then He had a church. The church exists for His mission.

Conclusion

Usually, when we see a sign that says "Danger" or "Beware" we take notice and avoid the problem. The problem here is that we often think we are smarter than we are, we know how to interpret the Bible, and we are confident that the lessons of the Bible might be out of touch, or not really applicable to modern times. John hung out such a danger sign "Whosoever transgresseth, and abideth not in the doctrine of

Christ, hath not God. He that abideth in the doctrine of Christ, he hath both the Father and the Son" (2 Jn. 9).

His warning was largely ignored, and now we have divisions in His church due to the logic of man, the reasoning of man, and the pride of man. Although the church may be in continual crisis, it has a constant stability.

Four themes exist that we should know about as we bring this study to a close.

1) We are in an age where people are completely consumed by expressive individualism.
2) In a society that relegates faith to the private world of self we have to be sensible about our view of religion and faith.
3) Not only are people seeing Christianity as old fashioned, but it is also being criticized as dangerous.
4) Even in this age of increased connectivity (the internet) we are increasingly disconnected, fragmented, and polarized.

<u>We study</u> doctrine not for the sake of doctrine itself, but for its application and the love of God's word for us. <u>We study</u> doctrine because it leads to love; to know God equips you to act in love. <u>We study</u> doctrine because it leads to humility; it reveals the distance between His holiness and our sinfulness. <u>We study</u> doctrine because it leads to obedience; we pursue Him and not cold facts.

Another context

"Freedom requires virtue, virtue requires faith, faith requires freedom." Os Guinness - *The Golden Triangle: A Free People's Suicide*

When I introduced this study, I offered an explanation about your responsibility as a citizen of heaven, a member of the Christian family. Part of that duty is to be a light on the hill, an example, and one of the best ways to be an example of Christ to others is to be a good citizen of your country. In doing so, you help others work through disagreements, tackle inequities, and do so in a loving way.

I am a history teacher, so I am going to claim a bit of academic license here for those who are citizens of the United States. The people who came here so many years ago were often trying to find a place to follow their own faith. Through their struggles they ended up creating our Constitution. It isn't a law that covers all situations, but a guiding precept for our daily laws, our social contract with one another to live and let live. One of the most basic foundations of that document is the freedom of religion. The Constitution was written for people of faith. In fact, it was assumed that people would understand that faith was the ground floor of government, and the basis of responsible self-governance. To quote Eric Mataxas "Our Constitution was made only for a moral and religious people." (p.61). When we discount faith in God, take mention of it out of our schools, remove all language of Him in our laws, and dare people to even mention His name in legal discourse, the foundation of what our country was created on crumbles. America was created for those who seek her blessings and want to live by her values. All are equal in God's sight…everyone. The gospel of Christ is the most powerful sociological level in history.

People will make much of the separation of church and state, but most of those arguments are made by people who are either ignorant of the meaning or who are doing their best to create dissention. All that was intended was an emphasis on the freedom of individual faith and denial of an official government church. If you didn't sleep through basic American history class, you know that religion enforced by the crown was what the early settlers were escaping. The major thing that makes self-governance work is the freedom of religion and its detachment from government.

Don't let those with divisive agendas drive your decisions. Think for yourself and know that your faith will strengthen this nation. It doesn't matter what your race is, what your bank account balance is, where you live, or what church you go to. The idea of self-governance assumes that we think for ourselves and for the good of others. We don't have to have an "us" versus "them" way of life here. Remember, do unto others as you would have them do unto you. We are all Americans.

Capacity to learn is a gift, Ability to learn is a skill, Willingness to learn is a choice…Brian Hebert

www.ingramcontent.com/pod-product-compliance
Lightning Source LLC
Chambersburg PA
CBHW020506160726
47991CB00007B/2829